22

D1179412

Countries qualifying for World Cup 82

The colours denote the five groups of countries, geographically based, which played in the qualifying competitions. Throughout pages 11 to 36, for easy reference, these colours are repeated when referring to a qualifying nation.

24

1	Italy	9	Argentina	17	Spain
2	Poland	10	Belgium	18	Honduras
3	Peru	11	Hungary	19	Yugoslavia
4	Cameroon	12	El Salvador	20	Northern Ireland
5	West Germany	13	England	21	Brazil
6	Austria	14	France	22	USSR
7	Chile	15	Czechoslovakia	23	Scotland
8	Algeria	16	Kuwait	24	New Zealand

A lasting, personal souvenir for all football fans — keep your own record of World Cup '82 as each round is played.

The book also contains plenty of information about previous World Cup finals and details of this year's tournament and the preparations in Spain.

Acknowledgments
The author and publishers wish to thank the following for additional illustrative material: page 26, All-Sport Photographic Ltd; pages 45, 46, Colorsport; front endpaper and flags, Drury Lane Studios, Solihull; maps by Roy Smith; page 34, Jack Spencer; page 36, Frank Spooner Pictures; pages 4, 5, 20, 23, 24, 25, 29, 30, 32, Syndication International Ltd.
Every effort has been made to trace copyright holders, and we apologise for any omissions.

First Edition

© LADYBIRD BOOKS LTD MCMLXXXII

WORLD CUP 82

written by JOHN P BAKER
designed by CHRIS REED

Ladybird Books Loughborough

How it all started

The Olympic Games provided world competition for amateur footballers but as the professional game grew throughout the world, FIFA, the organisation concerned with the administration of international football, wanted an equivalent competition for professional footballers. After ten years of discussion and planning, Jules Rimet, the president of the French Football Association and of FIFA, saw his dreams become reality with the staging of the 1930 World Cup finals. They were held in Uruguay, the country which had provided the Olympic champions in 1924 and 1928. Thirteen teams travelled from different parts of the world to contest the first World Cup competition. None of the British teams took part because they were not members of FIFA at the time.

Out of respect for all the work Jules Rimet had done to launch the competition, FIFA decided to name the trophy the *Jules Rimet Cup*. It was solid gold, 30 cm high and it weighed just over 4 kilograms.

Jules Rimet Cup

World travel is very quick and easy nowadays but it has not always been so. One of the early decisions a country had to make before entering the competition was whether it could afford to employ its players for the two months it could take to travel to the host country, play in the competition and then travel back. In 1934 and 1938 the whole competition was run on a knock-out basis and in 1934 the USA, Argentina and Brazil travelled all the way to Italy for just one match.

Since 1950, when the World Cup finals were held again after a break of twelve years for World War II, different ways have been tried to give each team more games. The sixteen teams were arranged in groups at first, with the successful teams in each group going on to a knock-out competition. The 1982 finals involve twenty-four teams for the first time ever.

The *Jules Rimet Cup* was played for until 1970 when Brazil, having won it three times, was allowed to keep it for ever. It might have been necessary to replace it sooner if a little dog called Pickles hadn't sniffed the *Jules Rimet Cup* out from under a laurel bush in his garden, after it had been stolen from a display in a stamp exhibition in London in 1966. Pickles *(right)* got a reward and a medal for his trouble.

The new FIFA trophy is solid gold, 36 cm high and is simply called the *World Cup*.

Country	*F	Won	R/up	3rd	4th
Brazil	11	1958 1962 1970	1950	1938 1978	1974
West Germany († as Germany)	9	1954 1974	1966	1934† 1970	1958
Italy	9	1934 1938	1970		1978
Mexico	8				
Uruguay	7	1930 1950			1954 1970
Argentina	7	1978	1930		
Hungary	7		1938 1954		
Sweden	7		1958	1950	1938
France	7			1958	
England	6	1966			
Czechoslovakia	6		1934 1962		
Yugoslavia	6			1930 §	1962
Switzerland	6				
Chile	5			1962	
Spain	5				1950
Belgium	5				
Netherlands	4		1974 1978		
Austria	4			1954	1934
Russia	4				1966
Bulgaria	4				
Rumania	4				
Scotland	4				

* = Finals   § = Joint with USA

47 different countries have participated in the 11 World Cup Final Competitions held so far.

Countries qualifying three times
Peru, USA (joint 3rd place 1930), Paraguay, Poland (3rd place 1966)

Countries qualifying once
Egypt, Cuba, Norway, Dutch East Indies, Turkey, Korea, Northern Ireland, Colombia, Wales, Portugal (3rd place 1974), Israel, Morocco, El Salvador, Haiti, Iran, Zaire, East Germany, Australia, Tunisia North Korea

Finals since 1930

Host Nation	World Champions	Runners-up
1930 Uruguay	Uruguay 4	Argentina 2
1934 Italy	Italy 2 (1-1) before extra time	Czecho'vakia 1
1938 France	Italy 4	Hungary 2
1950 Brazil	Final Pool Uruguay 5 points	Brazil 4 points
1954 Switzerland	W. Germany 3	Hungary 2
1958 Sweden	Brazil 5	Sweden 2
1962 Chile	Brazil 3	Czecho'vakia 1
1966 England	England 4 (2-2) before extra time	W. Germany 2
1970 Mexico	Brazil 4	Italy 1
1974 W. Germany	W. Germany 2	Holland 1
1978 Argentina	Argentina 3	Holland 1

The 1982 World Cup finals in Spain

Spain prepares

The World Cup finals will take place in seventeen stadiums in fourteen centres throughout Spain. Madrid, Barcelona and Seville will be using two stadiums each, the other towns will use only one. The grounds have all been renovated to meet the standards required for the competition and some have been enlarged considerably.

Some of the stadiums are owned by clubs we have heard of through European competitions. The opening match, three second round matches and the semi-final will take place at Nou Camp, the home of FC Barcelona. New floodlights have been installed there and its capacity has been expanded from 90000 to 120000 people, making it one of Europe's largest grounds.

Atletico Madrid's Stadium the Vicente Calderón, has only had to have minor renovations. Its 65 695 all-seater stadium will be used for three second round matches.

The stadium to stage the final and three second round matches belongs to Real Madrid. It is called Santiago Bernabeu and has been given a bigger roof to put three-quarters of the seats under cover. All the renovation work has actually reduced the capacity from 99 000 to 90 800 people but 35 800 of these will be seated.

A special footbridge 150 m long has been constructed over the Paseo de la Castellana to link the Bernabeu Stadium to the Congress Centre which will be the centre of activity for FIFA (see picture on back endpaper). The bridge will allow officials and press easy access between the stadium and the centre and cause less disruption to the traffic below. It has Madrid's coat of arms on both sides and after the competition it will be dismantled.

Spain's World Cup bus. Each team's bus will be painted in its national flag colours. The windscreen is over 2 m high and each bus contains thirty-five reclining seats, lounge space, a bar, a 'fridge, TV set, video recorder, hi-fi equipment, night lights and a bathroom

With centres all over Spain, quite a lot of travelling is involved. Each team will have its own special World Cup bus. It will be a *Pegasus 6100* with bodywork designed by the Van Hool factory in Zaragoza.

Twenty-six of these buses have been ordered as well as twenty-six mini-buses and twenty-six vans for luggage.

A lot of money is involved in arranging the World Cup. In Argentina in 1978, FIFA's turnover was just over £20 million. They estimate it will be twice that in Spain, with an expected income of £10 million from TV rights, £9 million from ground advertising, £7½ million from the sale of World Cup mascots and £12½ million from ground admission. It is expected that an average of 55 000 people will watch each of the fifty-two matches at the stadiums and, of course, thousands of millions will watch at home on television.

There should be plenty of people in Spain in June and July and just in case all the usual accommodation is filled, ships and trains are being transformed into hotels to cope with the visitors.

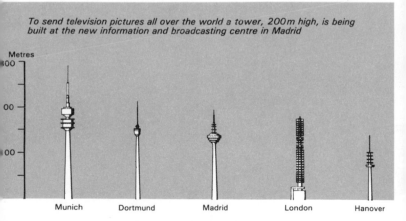

To send television pictures all over the world a tower, 200m high, is being built at the new information and broadcasting centre in Madrid

1 Brazil
2 Bolivia
3 Venezuela
4 Peru
5 Uruguay
6 Colombia
7 Chile
8 Ecuador
9 Paraguay
10 Argentina

The way to Spain

One hundred and eight countries entered teams in the 1982 FIFA World Cup, and only twenty-four teams could play in the finals in Spain. The teams were arranged in groups to play qualifying competitions. Spain – the hosts – and Argentina – the holders of the trophy – automatically qualified for the finals.

The five groups were geographically based to reduce the travelling. They were:

Host Country		
World Champions		
South America	9 entries	3 to qualify
North & Central America	15 entries	2 to qualify
Europe	33 entries	13 to qualify
Asia/Oceania	21 entries	2 to qualify
Africa	28 entries	2 to qualify
	108 entries	24 to qualify

South America
Qualifying Competition

Group 1	P	W	D	L	F:A	Pts
Brazil	4	4	0	0	11:2	8
Bolivia	4	1	0	3	5:6	2
Venezuela	4	1	0	3	1:9	2

Group 2	P	W	D	L	F:A	Pts
Peru	4	2	2	0	5:2	6
Uruguay	4	1	2	1	5:5	4
Colombia	4	0	2	2	4:7	2

Group 3	P	W	D	L	F:A	Pts
Chile	4	3	1	0	6:0	7
Ecuador	4	1	1	2	2:5	3
Paraguay	4	1	0	3	3:6	2

1 Canada
2 Mexico
3 USA
4 Honduras
5 El Salvador
6 Guatemala
7 Costa Rica

8 Panama
9 Cuba
10 Surinam
11 Guyana
12 Haiti
13 Trinidad
14 Antilles

North and Central America

Preliminary Round

Northern Zone

	P	W	D	L	F:A	Pts
Canada	4	1	3	0	4:3	5
Mexico	4	1	2	1	8:5	4
USA	4	1	1	2	4:8	3

Central Zone

	P	W	D	L	F:A	Pts
Honduras	8	5	2	1	15:5	12
El Salvador	8	5	2	1	12:5	12
Guatemala	8	3	3	2	10:2	9
Costa Rica	8	1	4	3	6:10	6
Panama	8	0	1	7	3:24	1

Caribbean Zone

Extra Preliminary Round on a home and away basis
Guyana beat Grenada 7:5 on aggregate

Group A	P	W	D	L	F:A	Pts
Cuba	4	3	1	0	7:0	7
Surinam	4	2	1	1	5:3	5
Guyana	4	0	0	4	0:9	0

Group B	P	W	D	L	F:A	Pts
Haiti	4	2	1	1	4:2	5
Trinidad & Tobago	4	1	2	1	1:2	4
Netherland Antilles	4	0	3	1	1:2	3

Qualifying Competition

	P	W	D	L	F:A	Pts
Honduras	5	3	2	0	8:1	8
El Salvador	5	2	2	1	2:1	6
Canada	5	1	3	1	6:6	5
Mexico	5	1	3	1	6:3	5
Cuba	5	1	2	2	4:8	4
Haiti	5	0	2	3	2:9	2

13

11 10

14

Europe

Group 1	P	W	D	L	F:A	Pts
W. Germany	8	8	0	0	33:3	16
Austria	8	5	1	2	16:6	11
Bulgaria	8	4	1	3	11:10	9
Albania	8	1	0	7	4:22	2
Finland	8	1	0	7	4:27	2

Group 2	P	W	D	L	F:A	Pts
Belgium	8	5	1	2	12:9	11
France	8	5	0	3	20:8	10
Eire	8	4	2	2	17:11	10
Holland	8	4	1	3	11:7	9
Cyprus	8	0	0	8	4:29	0

Group 3	P	W	D	L	F:A	Pts
USSR	8	6	2	0	20:2	14
Czecho'vakia	8	4	2	2	15:6	10
Wales	8	4	2	2	12:7	10
Iceland	8	2	2	4	10:21	6
Turkey	8	0	0	8	1:22	0

Group 4	P	W	D	L	F:A	Pts
Hungary	8	4	2	2	13:8	10
England	8	4	1	3	13:8	9
Rumania	8	2	4	2	5:5	8
Switzerland	8	2	3	3	9:12	7
Norway	8	2	2	4	8:15	6

Group 5	P	W	D	L	F:A	Pts
Yugoslavia	8	6	1	1	22:2	13
Italy	8	5	2	1	12:5	12
Denmark	8	4	0	4	14:11	8
Greece	8	3	1	4	10:13	7
Luxembourg	8	0	0	8	1:23	0

Group 6	P	W	D	L	F:A	Pts
Scotland	8	4	3	1	9:4	11
N. Ireland	8	3	3	2	6:3	9
Sweden	8	3	2	3	7:8	8
Portugal	8	3	1	4	8:11	7
Israel	8	1	3	4	6:10	5

Group 7	P	W	D	L	F:A	Pts
Poland	4	4	0	0	12:2	8
E. Germany	4	2	0	2	9:6	4
Malta	4	0	0	4	2:15	0

16

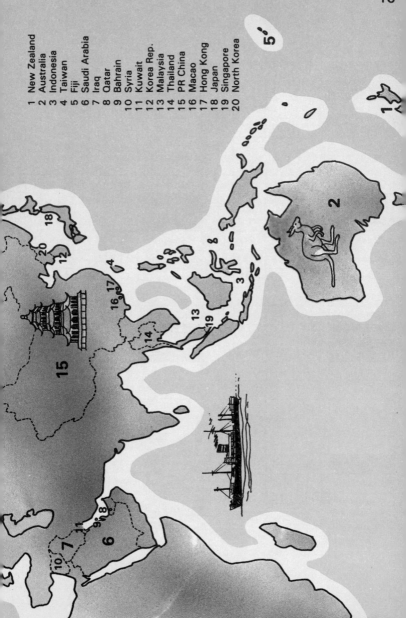

1 New Zealand
2 Australia
3 Indonesia
4 Taiwan
5 Fiji
6 Saudi Arabia
7 Iraq
8 Qatar
9 Bahrain
10 Syria
11 Kuwait
12 Korea Rep.
13 Malaysia
14 Thailand
15 PR China
16 Macao
17 Hong Kong
18 Japan
19 Singapore
20 North Korea

Asia/Oceania
Preliminary Round

Group 1
Played on a home and away
League basis

	P	W	D	L	F:A	Pts
New Zealand	8	6	2	0	31:3	14
Australia	8	4	2	2	22:9	10
Indonesia	8	2	2	4	5:14	6
Taiwan	8	1	3	4	5:8	5
Fiji	8	1	3	4	6:35	5

Group 2
Played as a tournament in
Saudi Arabia

	P	W	D	L	F:A	Pts
Saudi Arabia	4	4	0	0	5:0	8
Iraq	4	3	0	1	5:2	6
Qatar	4	2	0	2	5:3	4
Bahrain	4	1	0	3	1:6	2
Syria	4	0	0	4	2:7	0

Group 3
Played as a tournament in
Kuwait (Iran withdrew)

	P	W	D	L	F:A	Pts
Kuwait	3	3	0	0	12:0	6
Korea Rep.	3	2	0	1	7:4	4
Malaysia	3	0	1	2	3:8	1
Thailand	3	0	1	2	3:13	1

Group 4
Played as a tournament in
Hong Kong. Teams in the group:
*PR China, Macao, Hong Kong,
Japan, Singapore, North Korea*

Played as group matches:
semi-final : final

Final Result:
PR China 4 North Korea 2 after
extra time (2:2 at full time)

Qualifying Competition

	P	W	D	L	F:A	Pts
Kuwait	6	4	1	1	8:6	9
PR China	6	3	1	2	9:4	7
New Zealand	6	2	3	1	11:6	7
Saudi Arabia	6	0	1	5	4:16	1

Play-off match for second place
New Zealand 2 PR China 1

1 Libya
2 Gambia
3 Ethiopia
4 Zambia
5 Sierra Leone
6 Algeria
7 Senegal
8 Morocco
9 Guinea
10 Lesotho
11 Cameroon
12 Malawi
13 Tunisia
14 Nigeria
15 Uganda
16 Madagascar
17 Zaire
18 Mozambique
19 Niger
20 Somalia
21 Tanzania
22 Kenya
23 Ghana
24 Egypt
25 Zimbabwe
26 Sudan
27 Liberia
28 Togo

Africa

First Round: 2 legs
Libya Gambia
Ethiopia Zambia
Sierra Leone
Algeria
Senegal Morocco
Guinea Lesotho
Cameroon
Malawi
Tunisia Nigeria
Uganda — withdrew Madagascar
Zaire Mozambique
Niger Somalia
Tanzania Kenya
Ghana — withdrew Egypt

Second Round: 2 legs
Libya — withdrew Egypt
Algeria
Sudan
Niger Togo
Liberia Guinea
Cameroon
Zimbabwe
Morocco Zambia
Nigeria Tanzania
Madagascar Zaire

Third Round: 2 legs
Algeria
Niger
Guinea Nigeria
Morocco Egypt
Zaire
Cameroon

Qualifying Competition 2 legs

Algeria
Nigeria
Morocco
Cameroon

Byes: Zimbabwe
      Sudan
      Liberia
      Togo

South America

Argentina

Country
8th biggest country in the world
Population 27 million
Capital Buenos Aires — 6th largest city in the world
Currency 100 centaros = 1 Peso

Diego Maradona

Team
Manager Cesar Menotti — very experienced and well respected.

Players to watch
Diego Maradona, Mario Kempes, Osvaldo Ardiles

How they qualified
As World Champions

Previous appearances in finals
World Champions in 1978. Runners-up 1930, also played in finals in 1934, 1958, 1962, 1966, 1974. Beaten finalists in the first World Cup finals against old rivals Uruguay. Host nation in 1978 — 5th time the host nation won the trophy.

Registered number of footballers in the country 299 895.

Alternative colours
Dark blue

Team colours

South America
Peru

Country
Population 16 million   *Capital* Lima
Currency 100 centavos = 1 Sol

Team
Manager Elba de Padua – Brazilian

Players to watch Cubillas, Oblitas, Quiroga

How they qualified Defeating Uruguay and Colombia and drawing the other 2 matches.

Previous appearances in finals
1930, 1970, 1978.

Alternative colours
Red shirts, white shorts, white socks

South America
Chile

Country
Population 9 million   *Capital* Santiago
Currency 100 centavos = 1 Chilean Peso

Team
Manager Lois Santibanez

Players to watch Figuero, Caszely

How they qualified Defeated South American champions, Paraguay, twice to qualify. Won 3 and drew 1 of their 4 matches.

Previous appearances in finals
Third place in 1962 when hosts.
Other finals in 1930, 1950, 1966, 1974.

Alternative colours
All white

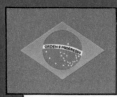

South America

Brazil

Country
5th biggest country in the world
Population 110 million
Capital Brasilia
Currency 100 centavos = 1 Cruzeiro

Zico

Team
Manager Tele Santana

Players to watch
Zico, Socrates, Junior
(Skilful and exciting team)

How they qualified
Won all 4 games of their
qualifying competition
scoring 11 goals and only
conceding 2.

*Previous appearances in
finals*
World Champions in 1958,
1962, 1970. Runners-up in
1950 (hosts).
Third place in 1938, 1978,
fourth place in 1974.
Played in finals in 1930,
1934, 1954, 1966.
The only country to play in
every World Cup finals. Won
the Jules Rimet Cup outright
in 1970.
Pele is the only player to
collect 3 World Cup
medals.

*Registered number of footballers in the
country* 112 755

*Team
colours*

Alternative colours
Blue shirts, white shorts, white socks

Europe

West Germany

Country
Population 61 million
Capital Bonn
Currency 100 pfennings = 1 Deutschemark

Rumenigge

Team
Manager Jupp Derwall

Players to watch
Rumenigge, Breitner, Briegel

How they qualified
Won all 8 games and scored
33 goals while only
conceding 3.

Previous appearances in finals
World Champions in 1954
and 1974 as hosts.
Runners-up 1966,
3rd place in 1934
(as Germany), 1970,
4th place in 1958 – other
finals 1938 (as Germany),
1962, 1978.

Registered number of footballers in the country 3 611 431

Alternative colours
Green shirts, white shorts, white socks

Team colours

Europe

Italy

Country
Population 56 million
Capital Rome
Currency Lire

Paolo Rossi

Team
Manager Enzo Bearzot

Players to watch
Roberto Bettega,
Paolo Rossi
(Very physical, hard tackling
team)

How they qualified
Runners-up to Yugoslavia in
qualifying competition,
winning 5 games and
drawing 2, out of 8.

---

*Previous appearances in
finals*
World champions in 1934.
As hosts in 1938.
Runners-up 1970. Fourth
place in 1978.
Other finals 1950, 1954,
1962, 1966, 1974.

*Registered number of footballers in the
country* 833 564

Alternative colours
White shirts, blue shorts, blue socks

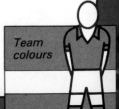

*Team
colours*

Europe

Scotland

Country
Population 5 million
Capital Edinburgh
Currency 100 pennies = 1 pound Sterling

Kenny Dalglish

Team
Manager Jock Stein

Players to watch
Kenny Dalglish, Graeme Souness, Steve Archibald

How they qualified
Won group competition winning 4 and drawing 3 of the 8 games.

Previous appearances in finals
1954, 1958, 1974, 1978.

Registered number of footballers in the country 109 000

Alternative colours
Red with stripes in dark blue

Team colours

Europe

USSR

Country
Biggest country in the world
Population 256 million — 3rd largest in the world
Capital Moscow — 7th largest city in the world
Currency 100 kopeks = 1 Rouble

Oleg Blokhin

Team
Manager
Konstantin Beskov

Players to watch
Oleg Blokhin, Alexander
Chivadze, Dassayev, Kipiani

How they qualified
Undefeated in qualifying.
Lead Group 3 by winning 6
and drawing 2 of their 8
games.

Previous appearances in finals
Fourth place in 1966.
Other finals 1958, 1962,
1970.

Registered number of footballers in the country 4 505 000

Alternative colours
All white

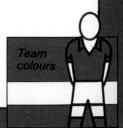

Team colours

Europe
Belgium

Country
Population 10 million   *Capital* Brussels
Currency 100 centimes = 1 Belgian franc

Team
Manager Guy Thys   *Players to watch* Van der Eycken, Coulmans, Van der Bergh, Van Moer.

How they qualified Group 2 winners in the qualifying competition, winning 5 games and drawing 1 out of 8.

Previous appearances in finals
1930, 1934, 1938, 1954, 1978.
One of the 13 teams in the first
World Cup finals.
Runners-up in 1980 European Championships.

Team colours

Alternative colours
Red shirts, black shorts, red socks

Europe
France

Country
Population 53 million   *Capital* Paris
Currency 100 centimes = 1 French franc

Team
Manager Mich Hidalgo   *Player to watch* Platini

How they qualified Runners-up to Belgium in Group 2 of the European competition. Won 5 games out of 8 and scored 20 goals.

Previous appearances in finals Third place in 1958. Other finals in 1930, 1934, 1938 (hosts), 1954, 1966, 1978. One of the 13 nations to compete in the first World Cup finals.

Team colours

Alternative colours
White shirts, blue shorts, red socks

Europe
Hungary

Country
Population 10 million *Capital* Budapest
Currency 100 filler = 1 Florint

Team
Manager Kalman Meszoly

Players to watch Nyilasi, Torocsik, Fazekas

How they qualified Won Group 4 in European competition. Won 4 and drew 2 of their 8 games.

Previous appearances in finals Runners-up in 1938, 1954. Other finals in 1934, 1958, 1962, 1966, 1978.

Team colours

Alternative colours
All white

Europe
Austria

Country
Population 7.5 million *Capital* Vienna
Currency 100 groschen = 1 Schilling

Team
Manager Karl Stotz

Players to watch Koncilia, Hans Krankl who scored 4 goals in 1978 finals.

How they qualified Runners-up to West Germany in Group 1 in Europe, won 5 games and drew 1.

Previous appearances in finals
Third place in 1954, fourth place in 1934. Other finals in 1938, 1978.

Team colours

Alternative colours
White shirts, black shorts, black socks

Europe

England

Country
Population 56 million
Capital London – 9th largest city in the world
Currency 100 pennies = 1 pound sterling

Kevin Keegan

Team
Manager Ron Greenwood

Players to watch
Kevin Keegan,
Trevor Francis,
goalkeepers – Shilton and
Clemence
(The England squad has an
average age of 30 and is an
experienced side)

How they qualified
Runners-up to Hungary in
European Group 4.

*Previous appearances in
finals*
World Champions and hosts
1966.
Other finals in 1950, 1954,
1958, 1962, 1970.

*Registered number of footballers in the
country* 505 000

Alternative colours
Red shirts, white shorts, red socks

*Team
colours*

Europe

Spain

Country
Population 36 million
Capital Madrid
Currency 100 centimos = 1 Peseta

Team
Manager Jose Santamaria

Players to watch
Zamora, Juanito
goalkeeper – Arconada
(The Spanish squad has an
average age of 25. This is
4 years younger than the
squad that played in
Argentina in 1978)

How they qualified
As the host nation.

*Previous appearances in
finals*
Fourth place in 1950.
Other finals in 1934, 1962,
1966, 1978.

Zamora

*Registered number of footballers in the
country* 202 574

Alternative colours
Blue shirts, blue shorts, black socks

*Team
colours*

Europe
Poland

Country
Population 34 million   *Capital* Warsaw
Currency 100 groszy = 1 Zloty

Team
Manager Antoni Piechniczek

Players to watch Lato, Szarmach

How they qualified Won European Group 7 defeating East
Germany and Malta, winning all 4 games and scoring 12 goals.

Previous appearances in finals
Third place in 1974. Other finals in
1938, 1978.

Team colours

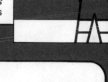

Alternative colours
Red shirts, white shorts, red socks

Europe
Czechoslovakia

Country
Population 15 million   *Capital* Prague
Currency 100 haleru = 1 Koruna

Team
Manager Josef Venglos

Player to watch Masny

How they qualified Runners-up to USSR in qualifying competition.
Won 4 out of 8 games and beat Wales only on goal difference.

Previous appearances in finals
Runners-up in 1934, 1962. Other finals in
1938, 1954, 1958, 1970. European Champions
1976. Olympic Champions 1980.

Team colours

Alternative colours
White shirts, white shorts, red socks

Europe

Northern Ireland

Country
Population 1.5 million
Capital Belfast
Currency 100 pennies = 1 pound Sterling

Pat Jennings

Team
Manager Billy Bingham

Players to watch
Pat Jennings, Martin O'Neill

How they qualified
Runners-up to Scotland
in European Group 6,
winning 3 and drawing 3 of
their 8 games.

Previous appearances in finals
1958.

Registered number of footballers in the country 17 685

Alternative colours
White shirts, green shorts, green socks

Team colours

Europe
Yugoslavia

Country
Population 21 million   *Capital* Belgrade
Currency 100 para = 1 Yugoslavian dinar

Team
Manager Miljan Miljanic

Players to watch Surjak, Halilbodzic

How they qualified Won European Group 5, winning 6 games and drawing 1 of their 8 games.

Previous appearances in finals
Joint third in 1930.
Fourth 1962. Other finals in
1950, 1954, 1958, 1974.

Alternative colours
White shirts, white shorts, red socks

Asia/Oceania
Kuwait

Country
Population 1 million   *Capital* Kuwait
Currency: 1000 fils = 1 Kuwaiti dinar

Team
Manager Carlos Alberto Parreire – (Brazilian)

Players to watch Faisal Al Dakheel, Ahmed Al Tarabulsy, Saad Al Houti

How they qualified Won group qualifying tournament in Kuwait and also the final group competition.

Previous appearances in finals
None.

Alternative colours
Red shirts, white shorts, red socks

Asia/Oceania
New Zealand

Country
Population 3 million   *Capital* Wellington
Currency 100 cents = 1 N.Z. Dollar

Team
Manager John Adshead

Player to watch Leading goalscorer Wynton Rufer – scored qualifying goal.

How they qualified Won preliminary competition winning 6 games and drawing 2 out of 8 and scoring 31 goals.
Joint runners-up with China in final group competition. Won the play-off.

Previous appearances in finals None

Wynton Rufer,
formerly with Norwich City

Registered number of footballers
in the country 41 698

Team
colours

Alternative colours
All white

Africa **Algeria**

Country
Population 18 million   *Capital* Algiers
Currency 100 centimes = 1 Algerian dinar

Team   *Manager* Yevgeni Rogor

Player to watch Kourichi

How they qualified Won 4 rounds of 2 legs each, in a knock-out competition.

Previous appearances in finals None

Team
colours

Alternative colours
All white

Africa
Cameroon

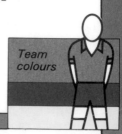

Team colours

Country
Population 7 million   *Capital* Yaounde
Currency African financial community franc

Team   *Manager* Branko Zutic – Yugoslav

Player to watch Milla

Previous appearances in finals None
                        Alternative colours
            Yellow shirts, green shorts, red socks

North and Central America
Honduras

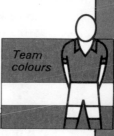

Team colours

Country
Population 3 million   *Capital* Tegucigalpa
Currency 100 centavos = 1 Lempira

Team   *Manager* Chelato Herrera

Player to watch Bailey

Previous appearances in finals None
                        Alternative colours
                                All white

North and Central America
El Salvador

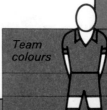

Team colours

Country
Population 4 million   *Capital* San Salvador
Currency 100 centavos = 1 Salvadorian colon

Team   *Manager* Mauricio Rodriguez

Player to watch Jorge Gonzales

Previous appearances in finals None

                        Alternative colours
                                All white

How they qualified See pages 13, 19.

Draw for the 1982 World Cup finals

There will be forty matches in the final tournament and these will be played between 13th June and 11th July. The early stages are not on a knock-out basis, because this could mean that a team had made all its preparations and gone to a lot of expense for just one game. Each team plays at least three games. Those going on to the second phase play five games, and the top four teams play seven games.

The teams were put into the draw on 16th January and arranged in six groups of four. In each group the teams play each other once and a league table is drawn up from the results. Twelve teams are eliminated, and twelve go on to the second phase. The successful teams are then arranged in four groups of three and play another series of matches. The four leaders in the second phase become semi-finalists. There is a third and fourth place play-off and the World Cup Final. The winners of the Final become the new World Champions.

The boys of the Colegio San Ildefonso prepare to assist with the draw

1 Italy	5 W. Germany	9 Argentina	13 England	17 Spain	21 Brazil
2 Poland	6 Algeria	10 Belgium	14 France	18 Honduras	22 USSR
3 Peru	7 Chile	11 Hungary	15 Czecho-slovakia	19 Yugoslavia	23 Scotland
4 Cameroon	8 Austria	12 El Salvador	16 Kuwait	20 N. Ireland	24 New Zealand

GROUP A
A1 A2 A3

GROUP B
B4 B5 B6

GROUP C
C7 C8 C9

GROUP D
D10 D11 D12

SEMI-FINALS
A C
B D

PLAY-OFF FOR THIRD AND FOURTH PLACE

FINAL

The results of the draw
The colour coding shows how the winners and runners-up in each group will progress through each round. For easy reference these colours are followed through on pages 39 to 49. You can complete this table as the tournament progresses.

World Cup diary

13th JUNE
Argentina v Belgium *(3)*

14th JUNE
Italy v Poland *(1)*
Brazil v USSR *(6)*

15th JUNE
Peru v Cameroon *(1)*
Hungary v El Salvador *(3)*
Scotland v New Zealand *(6)*

16th JUNE
West Germany v Algeria *(2)*
England v France *(4)*
Spain v Honduras *(5)*

17th JUNE
Chile v Austria *(2)*
Czechoslovakia v Kuwait *(4)*
Yugoslavia v Northern Ireland *(5)*

18th JUNE
Italy v Peru *(1)*
Argentina v Hungary *(3)*
Brazil v Scotland *(6)*

19th JUNE
Poland v Cameroon *(1)*
Belgium v El Salvador *(3)*
USSR v New Zealand *(6)*

20th JUNE
West Germany v Chile *(2)*
England v Czechoslovakia *(4)*
Spain v Yugoslavia *(5)*

21st JUNE
Algeria v Austria *(2)*
France v Kuwait *(4)*
Honduras v Northern Ireland *(5)*

22nd JUNE
Peru v Poland *(1)*
Belgium v Hungary *(3)*
USSR v Scotland *(6)*

23rd JUNE
Italy v Cameroon *(1)*
Argentina v El Salvador *(3)*
Brazil v New Zealand *(6)*

24th JUNE
Algeria v Chile *(2)*
France v Czechoslovakia *(4)*
Honduras v Yugoslavia *(5)*

25th JUNE
West Germany v Austria *(2)*
England v Kuwait *(4)*
Spain v Northern Ireland *(5)*

28th JUNE-5th JULY
Top two teams from each group
play in the second phase of the
competition

8th JULY
Semi-finals

10th JULY
Third place play-off

11th JULY
World Cup Final 1982

Figures in italics denote groups

GROUP 1	LA CORUÑA AND VIGO
GROUP 2	OVIEDO AND GIJÓN
GROUP 3	ELCHE AND ALICANTE
GROUP 4	VALLADOLID AND BILBAO
GROUP 5	ZARAGOZA AND VALENCIA
GROUP 6	SEVILLA AND MÁLAGA

The fourteen centres for World Cup games

Keep your own record of the 1982 World Cup Tournament

FA have modified their rules to permit each ountry to name its squad of players 30 days efore the start of the World Cup, instead of e customary 40 days.

Group 1

Italy
Poland
Peru
Cameroon

irst Round

		Score		Score
14th June at Vigo	Italy	☐	Poland	☐
15th June at La Coruña	Peru	☐	Cameroon	☐
18th June at Vigo	Italy	☐	Peru	☐
19th June at La Coruña	Poland	☐	Cameroon	☐
22nd June at La Coruña	Peru	☐	Poland	☐
23rd June at Vigo	Italy	☐	Cameroon	☐

Now fill in the results table: 2 points for a win   1 point for a draw

	Won	Drawn	Lost	Goals for	Goals against	Points

Group Winners _ _ _ _ _ _ _ _ _ _ _ _ _ _ _ _ _ _ (A1)

Runners-up _ _ _ _ _ _ _ _ _ _ _ _ _ _ _ _ _ _ (C7)

*ow enter these teams alongside **A1** on page 45 and **C7** on page 47 r the second phase of the competition.*

Group 2

West Germany

Algeria

Chile

Austria

Date		Score		Score
16th June *at Gijon*	W. Germany ☐		Algeria	☐
17th June *at Oviedo*	Chile ☐		Austria	☐
20th June *at Gijon*	W. Germany ☐		Chile	☐
21st June *at Oviedo*	Algeria ☐		Austria	☐
24th June *at Oviedo*	Algeria ☐		Chile	☐
25th June *at Gijon*	W. Germany ☐		Austria	☐

Now fill in the results table: 2 points for a win   1 point for a draw

	Won	Drawn	Lost	Goals for	Goals against	Points

Group Winners _____ (B4)

Runners-up _____ (D10)

*Now enter these teams alongside **B4** on page 46 and **D10** on page 48 for the second phase of the competition.*

Group 3

- Argentina
- Belgium
- Hungary
- El Salvador

Date		Score		Score
13th June at Barcelona	Argentina		Belgium	
15th June at Elche	Hungary		El Salvador	
18th June at Alicante	Argentina		Hungary	
19th June at Elche	Belgium		El Salvador	
22nd June at Elche	Belgium		Hungary	
23rd June at Alicante	Argentina		El Salvador	

Now fill in the results table: 2 points for a win   1 point for a draw

	Won	Drawn	Lost	Goals for	Goals against	Points

Group Winners _____ (A3)

Runners-up _____ (C9)

Now enter these teams alongside A3 on page 45 and C9 on page 47 or the second phase of the competition.

First Round

Group 4

England

Czechoslovakia

France

Kuwait

Date		Score		Score
16th June at Bilbao	England	3	France	1
17th June at Valladolid	Czechs		Kuwait	
20th June at Bilbao	England		Czechs	
21st June at Valladolid	France		Kuwait	
24th June at Valladolid	France		Czechs	
25th June at Bilbao	England		Kuwait	

Now fill in the results table: 2 points for a win   1 point for a draw

	Won	Drawn	Lost	Goals for	Goals against	Points
England	✓			3	1	2

Group Winners _ (B6)

Runners-up _ (D12)

*Now enter these teams alongside **B6** on page 46 and **D12** on page 48 for the second phase of the competition.*

Group 5

Spain

Honduras

Yugoslavia

N. Ireland

Date		Score		Score
16th June *at Valencia*	Spain	☐	Honduras	☐
17th June *at Zaragoza*	Yugoslavia	☐	N. Ireland	☐
20th June *at Valencia*	Spain	☐	Yugoslavia	☐
21st June *at Zaragoza*	Honduras	☐	N. Ireland	☐
24th June *at Zaragoza*	Honduras	☐	Yugoslavia	☐
25th June *at Valencia*	Spain	☐	N. Ireland	☐

Now fill in the results table: 2 points for a win   1 point for a draw

	Won	Drawn	Lost	Goals for	Goals against	Points

Group Winners _ (D11)

Runners-up _ (B5)

*Now enter these teams alongside **D11** on page 48 and **B5** on page 46 for the second phase of the competition.*

Group 6

Brazil

USSR

Scotland

New Zealand

Date	Team	Score	Team	Score
14th June *at Sevilla*	Brazil		USSR	
15th June *at Málaga*	Scotland		New Zealand	
18th June *at Sevilla*	Brazil		Scotland	
19th June *at Málaga*	USSR		New Zealand	
22nd June *at Málaga*	USSR		Scotland	
23rd June *at Sevilla*	Brazil		New Zealand	

Now fill in the results table: 2 points for a win   1 point for a draw

	Won	Drawn	Lost	Goals for	Goals against	Points

Group Winners _ _ _ _ _ _ _ _ _ _ _ _ _ _ _ _ _ _ **C8**

Runners-up _ **A2**

*Now enter these teams alongside **C8** on page 47 and **A2** on page 45 for the second phase of the competition.*

Second Round
Group A

*To be played in
Nou Camp, Barcelona
(below)*

(A1) _____

(A2) _____

(A3) _____

	Score		Score
28th June _____	☐	_____	☐
1st July _____	☐	_____	☐
4th July _____	☐	_____	☐

Now fill in the results table: 2 points for a win   1 point for a draw

	Won	Drawn	Lost	Goals for	Goals against	Points

Group Winners _____ **A**

Now enter this team alongside A in the Semi-final on page 49.

Second Round
Group B

*To be played in
Santiago Bernabeu,
Madrid (below)*

(B4) _____

(B5) _____

(B6) _____

	Score				Score	

29th June _____ ☐ _____ ☐

2nd July _____ ☐ _____ ☐

5th July _____ ☐ _____ ☐

Now fill in the results table: 2 points for a win   1 point for a draw

	Won	Drawn	Lost	Goals for	Goals against	Points

Group Winners _____ **B**

Now enter this team alongside B in the Semi-final on page 49.

Second Round
Group C

*To be played in
Sarriá, Barcelona
(below)*

C7 _____

C8 _____

C9 _____

	Score		Score
29th June _____	☐	_____	☐
2nd July _____	☐	_____	☐
5th July _____	☐	_____	☐

Now fill in the results table: 2 points for a win   1 point for a draw

	Won	Drawn	Lost	Goals for	Goals against	Points

Group Winners _____ **C**

*Now enter this team alongside **C** in the Semi-final on page 49.*

Second Round
Group D

To be played in
Vicente Calderón,
Madrid (below)

 D10 _____

 D11 _____

D12 _____

		Score				Score	
28th June _____		☐		_____			☐
1st July _____		☐		_____			☐
4th July _____		☐		_____			☐

Now fill in the results table: 2 points for a win   1 point for a draw

	Won	Drawn	Lost	Goals for	Goals against	Points

Group Winners_____ **D**

Now enter this team alongside D in the Semi-final on page 49

Semi-finals of the competition

8th July *at Nou Camp, Barcelona*

	Score		Score
A _____	☐	**C** _____	☐

Goal Scorers: Goal Scorers:

Enter winners _____ in the final
on page 51

Enter losers _____ in 3rd & 4th place play-off
on page 50

8th July *at Sánchez Pizjuan, Sevilla*

	Score		Score
B _____	☐	**D** _____	☐

Goal Scorers: Goal Scorers:

Enter winners _____ in the final
on page 51

Enter losers _____ in 3rd & 4th place play-off
on page 50

Third and fourth place play-off

10th July *at José Rico Pérez, Alicante*

Score

Score

_ _ _ _ _ _ _ _ _ _ _ _ _ _   _ _ _ _ _ _ _ _ _ _ _ _

Players   **Players**

Substitutes   **Substitutes**

Goal Scorers   **Goal Scorers**

Winners _ _ _ _ _ _ _ _ _ _ _ _ _ _ _ _ _ take 3rd place in
the competition

Losers _ _ _ _ _ _ _ _ _ _ _ _ _ _ _ _ _ take 4th place in
the competition

World Cup Final Spain 1982

11th July *at Santiago Bernabeu, Madrid*

Score

Score

_ _ _ _ _ _ _ _ _ _ _   _ _ _ _ _ _ _ _ _ _ _

Players   **Players**

Substitutes   **Substitutes**

Goal Scorers   **Goal Scorers**

World Champions 1982 _ _ _ _ _ _ _ _ _ _ _ _ _ _ _

Runners-up _